ANDY JACKSON'S WATER WELL

Andy Jackson's Water Well

WILLIAM O. STEELE

Illustrated by Michael Ramus

HARCOURT, BRACE AND COMPANY, NEW YORK

LIBRARY OF CONGRESS CATALOG CARD NUMBER: 59-7282
PRINTED IN THE UNITED STATES OF AMERICA

ANDY JACKSON'S WATER WELL

One

Now in those days the town of Nashville was hardly there at all. It was just a fistful of log cabins and a crookedy cowpath. And all around, the great trees rose up green and full, the streams ran and sparkled, and the bear and deer played wood tag in the clover bottoms.

But one day a long, tall figure came riding into town on an old black horse. He was a pale young man with a nose sharp enough to skin a deer with, though he hardly ever had. His eyes were blue and he had hair as red as a brush fire, with a temper to match. He brought with him some

7

dusty books, a great many goose-quill pens, and a very small silver mill for grinding peppercorns.

This young feller tied his horse to a sweet gum tree and moved into one of the log cabins. He put his quills upon the table, his books upon the fireboard shelf beside the silver pepper mill.

Then he went outside and nailed up a sign that said:

ANDREW JACKSON
ATTORNEY-AT-LAW
Honest Ranting——Reliable Bellowing
Wrathy Arguments Settled Cheap

After that Andy went back inside and waited for somebody who wanted to go a-lawing. He waited quite a spell, but nobody came.

He read through all his law books, but nobody seemed to care that he knew the difference between a bristly Latin verb and a chinquapin bur, between a mule's pulley bone and a hung jury. He chewed up all his goose-quill pens, but nobody in all Nashville needed a lawyer.

Andy was a little peeved. "For," he thought, "I came here to be a lawyer and to help out the folks with their troubles. But how can I be a lawyer if folks won't go to lawing?"

And he banged his fist on the table. "Something will have to be done," he cried.

So he took three buckets and filled them with sunshine. He brought them into the cabin and spread the sunlight neatly around the room. Of course he had to take three piggins of darkness outside and bury them by a blackberry bush.

"For in truth," said Andy, "my cabin has been so dim and dark, folks hadn't known I was here a-tall."

Now they could see him plain as a ladybug in a squash blossom, and they watched while Andy mended the fire and took out the ashes and swept the hearth with a turkey wing. He dusted the sycamore fluff and the fish scales and stick-tights off the books and the table and the stools. He polished the silver sides of the pepper mill.

After that he went out and shot a goose. He plucked it and sharpened some of the feathers for fresh quills. Then he put the goose on a spit to roast for supper. He took a bucket and filled it with cool spring water and set it by the door with a long-handled gourd floating across it.

By this time it was growing dark and Andy was getting tired, so he ate his supper, carried out the three piggins full of sunlight and toted in three buckets of darkness, wrapped himself in his blanket, and lay down on the warm hearth to sleep.

Next morning he woke up and looked around. His cabin was dim and dusty and dark again, and he could see that all those many things needed to be done over.

"Now," said Andy, "this will never do. If I spend my

time dusting and polishing, toting and fetching, there'll be no time for lawing. I must get somebody to help me."

So he put on a clean shirt and a pair of deerskin breeches and went out into the street. And the very first person he met was an Indian, a short, fat Indian wearing a blue blanket and carrying a bow and arrow tied up in the hair on top of his head.

"How!" greeted Andy. "What is your name and are you for hire?"

"And a great big how back to you," spoke the Indian. "My name is Chief Eight Shillings Six Pence Ticklepitcher. And whether I'm for hire depends upon the wages."

"I'll pay two fawn skins, a copper sovereign, and enough vermilion war paint to cover a horn spoon every month," Andy answered.

"Done and done!" cried the Chief, and they shook hands on the bargain.

Andy took Chief Ticklepitcher back to his office. And every day Chief Ticklepitcher cooked the meals and swept the hearth. He filled the ink well every morning and chopped the kindling wood. Come every Thursday he shot a goose to roast for supper and for quill pens. He entertained Andy's old black horse, so the critter wouldn't get lonely.

And every morning he brought in the sunlight and every evening he carried it out again. And when the cabin was dark of a night, he and Andy lay down on the warm hearth and slept.

As for Andy, he was busy as a mouse in a meal bag. The folks in Nashville began lawing left and right, for they had seen what an industrious young man he was. Now he had time to attend to their affairs, writing wills and deeds and documents at a great rate.

Day and night Andy worked away, writing with his quill pen on thick sheets of parchment and saying great long Latin words and dropping big blobs of sealing wax on official papers. But Andy was not quite content.

"For," he told himself, "there ought to be some fine great thing I could do for the good people of Nashville."

He complained to Chief Ticklepitcher.

"I would like to do something spondulacious for these folks," Andy said. "I would like to get an extra-powerful, fine law passed to make them prosperous and happy. Or I should like to make a most wise, solemn judgment that would help them in every kind of way, for they have been mighty good to me and I would like to do something to show them how much I think of them."

The Chief pondered for a while. "I can't think of a solitary thing," he replied. "Howsomever, I wouldn't be surprised if you can't figure out something grand."

But though Andy thought hard, he couldn't stumble on anything wonderful to do for the Nashville folks.

The days went sailing by, and the summer sun began to shine down on Nashville as bright as brass. The leaves of the trees hung limp and dull, and every little breeze made dust devils skitter up and down the streets.

"It's mighty dry weather," said Chief Ticklepitcher, and he hung a little medicine bag full of dead rat tails and powdered button snakeroot in the doorway to bring rain.

"Oh, it ain't nothing to worry about yet," replied Andy. "Some summers is just naturally dry."

But in truth he had already begun to worry some, and he wondered what would happen to the town if the dry weather continued.

The sun shone down hotter and hotter and brighter and brighter every day. The folks of Nashville looked everywhere for a black cloud, but there was none to see. No thunder rumbled, no lightning flashed, no cool sweet rain slashed down upon the roofs. No fine gray fog rose up from the river and trickled down the street. In the mornings no dew lay along the grass stems like big glass beads. And even the moonlight was hot.

"Folks is having a hard time," said Chief Ticklepitcher.

"Oh, I *know* they're having a mighty rough time of it," answered Andy, putting down his quill pen. "If I was a rain maker, I would make haste to bring the finest kind of rain."

Wells dried up and springs went plumb dry. The corn burned black in the fields. Little baby turtles swam in dusty puddles, for they'd never in their lives seen a drop of water. Folks took to squeezing their springs to get the last drop of water for their young 'uns.

Things got worse, and Andy *did* begin to worry. He paced back and forth in front of his office till his shadow wore a deep rut in the ground.

Chief Ticklepitcher did a rain-calling dance, and he gave Andy some powdered snail shells to wear in his boot to bring wet weather. But no drops fell.

The shingles on the roofs curled up in the terrible heat. Leather hinges became so dry, they squeaked like a cata-mount in a canebrake. The chinking between the cabin logs shrank and dropped out in great chunks. Cows and horses and pigs grew so thin, they dassn't cross the bridge for fear of slipping between the logs and falling into the dry creek below.

And then one day an old man came to Andy's office with a great bundle on his back.

13

ANDREW JACKSON
ATTORNEY-AT-LAW
Honest Ranting ~ Reliable Bellowing
Wrathy Arguments Settled Cheap

"I want you to write a deed for my home place," he told Andy, "for I'm leaving Nashville and I aim to sell it."

"Oh, don't do that," begged Andy. "Nashville is too fine a place to go off and leave."

"It *is* a fine place. But I can't stand this dry weather any longer," shouted the old man. "Why, looky here!"

He pointed to the bulge in his jaw. "I started chewing this wad of tobaccy in corn-planting time, and here it is September and it's been so dry all that time I ain't been able to spit yet."

"Oh, I know all you good folks have had hardships," said Andy, nodding. "And I hate it terribly."

"Well, Andy, it's plumb time to leave. It's so dry around here, when fish swim up the Cumberland River, they raise a cloud of dust," the old man went on. "It's so all-fired dry that when a man shoots a deer, he don't have to bother to jerk the meat. It's already done been dried for him."

"Here, now, wait," exclaimed Andy, whirling around like a dust devil himself. "Something must sure be done about this dry weather *right now*. Let's call all the folks together and see what we can figure out."

So Chief Ticklepitcher ran from cabin to cabin and soon all the folks of Nashville were gathered in the square. And when they were all listening, Andy cried out, "Now we can't let this drought drive us away from here, lock, stock, and water bucket. We must beat this dry weather! If anybody's got a notion what should be done, let him speak up."

"Make a bodacious speech, Andy!" cried one.

"Lead a wolfish, rip-snorting parade, Andy!" cried another.

"Nay," Andy answered. "Speeches are dry and parades are dusty. They wouldn't help at all."

So the folks thought and a few confabulated together.

"Write a law against droughts," shouted someone at last.

"Get out a search warrant for the equinox," yelled another.

"Oh, those are good things to do," Andy answered. "And I'll do them, for that's a lawyer's duty. But I don't reckon they'll be a heap of help, now the dry weather is already here."

So once more folks put their heads together and talked and worried and pondered prodigiously.

"Ain't there a cave near here we could stuff all this dry weather into?" some of them asked.

"No, I misdoubt there's a cave anywhere big enough to hold all this dry weather," answered Andy.

"There sure ain't, there sure ain't," cried out the Chief.

"If we had enough windmills, we could start them all going at once and blow this dry weather away," suggested Andy. "But I don't reckon there's that many windmills in the whole United States."

"Oh, you're right, you're most certainly right," hollered Chief Ticklepitcher.

"Well, what shall we do, Andy?" pleaded the folks of Nashville.

Now Andy figured he was smart enough to think up an answer to this problem. He put his hands in his pockets to help him think and he thought good and hard.

"I hear there's a heap of water in East Tennessee," Andy said finally.

"Oh, aye," answered the Chief. "Just a heap."

"And I reckon the onliest thing to do is go over there and fetch some of that water back to Nashville," Andy told them.

"That's the onliest thing," agreed Chief Ticklepitcher, and the people all nodded.

"So who'll volunteer to go over there and fetch us back some water?" asked Andy. "Some farmer can spare the time, for there's no crops to be got in. Or some fisherman, for there's no fish left and no rivers."

"We'd rather have you," cried the people. "You go."

"Me?" yelled Andy, most shocked and surprised. "Why, I'm a lawyer. I don't know beans about fetching water from any place. Lawing is all in this world I know. I'm powerful good at thinking up laws and reading in law books and writing up wills. But let somebody who knows more about such things get the water."

But the folks all wanted him to go. And Andy saw they did, for certain. He wasn't sure he'd be much good at it. But somebody had to go and he was glad to try.

"I'll do it," he told the Chief, "for it won't take long. And maybe as we journey along, I can think up some wonderful and helpful laws to get passed for these good people as soon as I get back home."

So Andy tidied up his quill pens and put out a leaf or two of assefedita to keep the fish weevils out of his law books. He ground a handful of peppercorns in his silver mill and filled a little pouch with the fine pepper.

Then he and Chief Ticklepitcher mounted their horses. And the folks of Nashville came to wish them "Fare-thee-well!" and "Good luck!"

Some of them called out words of advice and helpfulness, and many of them warned Andy to be on the lookout for Land Pirates, for these are the wickedest and hatefulest robbers in creation.

Andy thanked the folks and promised to be careful. He headed his horse east and galloped out of the settlement with the Chief at his side.

Two

Now as Andy and Chief Ticklepitcher rode eastward, Andy was feeling pretty hopeful. "For," he told himself, "very soon we'll reach East Tennessee where there is just a heap of water and I can try to fetch some back quick. And I most certainly hope I can do it, for, if I don't, folks will leave Nashville before I have a chance to show them how much I think of them."

They rode along and along and along the dusty road. On both sides the dry weather was stacked up in the fields like piles of logs. And sometimes it drifted across the road so thick and deep, the horses could hardly wade through it and Andy had to hold his feet high up out of the way.

"Oh, this here is a sad and sorry sight," Andy said to the Chief.

Log cabins and cowsheds and tobacco barns lay all twisted and withered and useless from the great heat. Once a fine river had run beside the road, but now it was shriveled and empty and browned terribly by the sun. Every now and then a big dry piece of it broke off and rolled away. And Andy looked sharp at every piece to make sure it wasn't a Land Pirate.

And all around, the countryside was bare and empty. There wasn't even a turkey buzzard in the sky, nor so much as a lizard skittering about on the ground. And not a spider, nor a piece of chickweed could be seen on the hard, cracked earth crust.

The sun shone hotter and hotter, brighter and brighter. The edges of the road curled up and turned black and leathery, and the hills on both sides began to droop and slide sideways.

After a spell Andy spoke up. "I'm dry. I'm parched as corn."

"It's a bad thing to be," answered the Chief, and he straightened the bow and arrow he carried in his hair.

They had not jogged more than a mile further when the trees began to melt like wax candles. A hot drop fell on the back of Andy's neck and almost made him mad.

"I want you to know I got a bad temper," he told the Chief. "But I aim to try hard not to lose it on this journey, for it takes up a heap of time. And I want to get this water business out of my way quick and get back home."

"Indians carry two red onions in their saddlebags and never get mad," said Chief Ticklepitcher, and Andy allowed he would have to try it.

The sun poured down and the heat waves shimmered up to meet it, thick as flour gravy. Andy and the Chief rode on at a right good clip, keeping an eye out for Land Pirates.

"I'm hot!" exclaimed Andy. "I'm so hot, my pockets are fried on both sides."

"Oh, that's the kind of thing that happens in this kind of weather," answered the Chief.

They rode on further without a pause.

"Now there's a spring," pointed Andy. "And I must have a drink out of it."

He got off his horse and walked over to the spring and bent down to drink. But just at that very moment a little wind came blowing along and whirled that dry and dusty spring away like dandelion fluff.

In spite of all he could do, Andy felt himself getting mad, mad for a fact. His elbows popped loudly and his shinbones crackled. He jumped up and down fiercely, till the ground rattled like corn shucks.

"I got to have a drink of water!" Andy bawled. "My tongue is swelled up big as a cannon. My throat is so dry, I dassn't turn my head for fear it will break off. Now I must have some water, for it's plumb dangerous for red-haired fellows like me to do without. Why, I'm liable to get so dry, I'll set myself afire and blaze up like a pine knot."

The Chief figured this might very well be true, and he tried hard to think of some way to calm Andy down. "Now you get back on your horse and I'll show you a way to ride that will keep you cooler," he said.

And he started off down the road, riding about a foot or two in the air above his horse's back. "It's much cooler this way," he told the lawyer.

But try as he might, Andy could not ride up in the air in that fashion. "It ain't no trouble to get up there," explained Andy. "The trouble is that once I get up there, I slide right off."

And the Chief told him it was because his mammy didn't feed him a soup made of cockleburs when he was young, for that enabled a body to stick to anything.

"Well, I'll ride underneath my horse," said Andy. "At least it's shady down under there."

So he turned his stirrups upside down and rode along easy as you please underneath his horse. But it became powerful hot and dusty after a while. Then Andy tried riding sidesaddle and riding on one hand and riding along behind, clinging to his horse's tail. But none of these helped. He was as tarnal thirsty and miserable as ever.

Howsomever, along about the middle of the afternoon, they came to a great deep gorge. And there at the very

bottom lay a river, though it was now just a little bare muddy trickle of water. Still it looked mighty handsome and delicious to Andy.

"We must have some of that water," he told Chief Ticklepitcher, licking his cracked lips. "We need it and the horses need it bad too."

The Chief shook his blanket to get the dust out of it. "That water is not likely to be very wet," he said.

"Well, it can't be too dry," replied Andy, "or it wouldn't be water."

"It may be you're right," nodded the Indian. "But how do you aim to get it for us?"

Andy looked back at the gorge. The sides were too steep to climb down and the water was too far away to reach by lowering a bucket.

"It's a problem," he admitted. "And young as I am, I'm not a-tall sure I know what to do."

Andy walked back and forth, kicking at all the pebbles, studying hard about it. At last he gave a shout and hurried to his saddlebag. He took out a telescope. "This here will surely do the trick for us," he said.

And he went up to the rim of the gorge and looked down at the river with the telescope. The telescope brought the water right up close to the edge where he stood.

"Now be quick and drink," he told the Chief, "for this spyglass is not very powerful and it won't hold this water up here very long."

So Chief Ticklepitcher had some. Then Andy drank. The water was only wet on one side. Andy drank a power of it and he was only half as thirsty as he had been before. But the horses would hardly touch the stuff.

"We got to get them critters some decent water to drink or they'll die for sure," Andy said.

It was true the horses looked bad off, so the two travelers gave them a short rest and then rode slowly toward the east once again. But the horses were well-nigh worn to a frazzle by the heat waves and the hot wind and the roasting sun.

Andy could see they couldn't go on much longer. He got off his old black horse and took off all the animals' shoes, which were heavy and half melted and so almighty sticky, the poor beasts could hardly raise their feet off the ground.

This helped some, and the horses eased along right pertly for a spell. Then they began to slow down and hang their heads and drag their feet once more. Andy studied what he could do to help them, for he hated worse than sin to see the animals suffer.

"It's them dern shadows," he told Chief Ticklepitcher. "The sun is so hot and bright and casts such thick old heavy shadows, they weigh on the poor critters something terrible. I'll just have to see can I get them shadows loosened up somehow."

So once more Andy got down. He took a piece of fat meat out of his saddlebag and rubbed it along the edge of the horses' hoofs, right smack at the place where the shad-

ows clung on. Of course, when the hoofs were all greasy like that, the shadows just slipped off, easy as you please, and they didn't weigh and pull on the poor beasts and slow them down any longer.

Andy felt mighty set up now, for he could see the long blue line of the Cumberland Mountains rising up against the sky. He made sure the horses would be able to finish the journey in good style.

But it grew hotter and hotter and man and beast got thirstier and thirstier. The sun was fierce as a wolf's tooth.

Andy and the Chief got off and led their horses, for the critters could hardly walk a step with burdens on their backs. And finally even this was too much for Andy's old black. He fell over in the dust and a tear trickled down his nose, for he was mighty sorry to let Andy down in this fashion.

"Oh, dear and oh, dear!" cried Chief Ticklepitcher. "I reckon we must all die out here in this desert, Andy, for the horses can't carry us and we surely can't tote them."

"No, I reckon not," agreed Andy sadly, and he patted his horse. "But I ain't going to forsake them."

"Then I best sit down and wait the end," sighed the Chief.

"No, you don't," cried Andy. "We ain't going to give up neither, for I have promised to bring back water and I mean to try a heap harder than this."

He stood on one foot and held the other one up to cool a bit and figured mightily. Though Andy was uneasy when he was away from his quill pens and his law books, still he was a powerful figurer at any time.

"You can see for yourself we're almost there," pointed out Andy. "Yonder's a bush or two and over there's a blade of grass, so take off your blanket."

The Chief spread out his blanket on the ground. And

27

then Andy made his old horse lie down on it and the Chief's horse too.

"Grab that end, Chief," Andy said. "And I'll take this 'un."

Then both of them began to pull. The blanket slid right easily over the hard-baked ground, and the horses rode along like ladies in a fine carriage.

Andy looked left and right for a spring, for though he and the Chief were both strong and vigorous, he knew they could not go on pulling the horses unless they soon had some water.

Now more and more shrubs grew by the wayside and little gnarled sapling trees and a heap of blackberry runners. Lizards sat under bushes swelling their little gullets in and out and eating ants by the fistful. A July fly went buzzing over Andy's head, and by and by they came to a tee-niny spring gurgling up between two rocks, and it made a sound as sweet as thrushes singing in the early days of April.

"We'll let the horses drink first," said Andy, "for they have been brave, good critters and they need water worse than us."

So the horses drank. And they drank that little spring plumb up! When they lifted their heads, there wasn't a thing left but a dab of mud and an angleworm. Andy's horse spit out a little young crawdad and it crawled away.

Andy was flabbergasted. "Why I'd counted on a drink of that water, for I'm pretty dry myself," he told the Chief. He turned sort of red and speckly all over with the effort of holding his temper.

"If I had me a legislature here, I'd pass a law against undersized springs like that," he groaned. "They make it powerful hard for a red-haired man to keep his temper."

"I can see it's powerful hard for you, but you're a-doing it, Andy," admired the Chief.

Andy wrestled a minute or two with his anger and then said, "Well, let's get on, for there's bound to be another spring some place close by."

The horses were strong enough to get up and walk now. The Chief put on his blanket and they journeyed on. Soon there were tall trees all around and cool shade to walk in and soft green grass underfoot.

They went on and on, and by and by came to a great river, full to the very top with clear water. In fact, it was so full that the top was way over Andy's head and he couldn't get a drink at all, no matter how he strained and stretched.

Now the sight and sound and smell of all that good fresh water so close was enough to drive them all into conniptions. The Chief tried hard to lift himself up by the hair on top of his head. The horses tried to stand on each other's back.

Some cane was growing close to the riverbank, yellow-green and tall as a tree. Andy saw that cane and it gave him a notion. He cut four of those canes and hollowed out the joints and made them into long straws. Then he and the Chief and the horses could stand on the ground and drink easily out of the top of that very full river.

Andy just drank a sip or two at first, for he well knew that when a body is terribly hot and dry, he should never drink a heap of cold water. Not only will it steam up his innards bodaciously, it will warp his joints and even spring a leak in his seams.

Howsomever, Chief Ticklepitcher didn't take it slow and easy. He just drank and drank.

Andy grabbed him by his blanket. "Now hold on a minute," he cried. "You must just drink a little mite when you are so hot and thirsty, else you will get flambastulated and comminxelled."

The Chief shook his head. "That only works for white

men," he told Andy. "It don't work for Injuns, for no matter how hot an Injun gets on the outside, he stays cool on the inside."

And though he drank very hearty, it was true he didn't have a single warped joint or cracked seam or get flambastulated in any way. Andy was always glad to learn something new about folks, for he was terribly young and ignorant, so he drank his water just a weensy bit at a time and cooled off slowly and thought about all he had to learn in this world.

And by and by he was as cool as a cabbage leaf, and he leaned back against a tree and looked around at all the beautiful green trees and bushes. And way over to one side he saw a heap of snakes playing guessing games and confabulating around. Oh, it was easy seen they were having a gay frolic!

"Why, they're grabbing their tails in their jaws and rolling like wheels," Andy cried. "If that don't beat all. I must get a closer look."

And he walked over to the little meadow where the snakes were circling about, cutting fancy figures and weaving in and out between the dog-hobble bushes.

Suddenly one of the snakes started rolling right at Andy.

"Run!" shouted the Chief. "It's a hoopsnake and he has a terrible fierce-killing stinger in his tail."

Three

Now Andy didn't waste time. Being only a town lawyer, he'd never seen a hoopsnake before, but he'd heard a huge heap about 'em. All the folks around Nashville said that hoopsnakes were the most wickedest, deadliest, meanest varmints in creation.

One drop of poison from the snake's stinger and a body turned green with mortification, swelled right up, and died in great agony. The very thought sent a bump of fear rising up in Andy's neck big as a goose egg.

Andy gave a quick running jump and took off. But he

didn't in reason see how he could get away, for hoopsnakes can roll faster than most red-haired lawyers can think, which is pretty fast indeed.

He shot by the spring and saw the Chief climbing up a grapevine like a hungry 'coon after birds' eggs. But Andy didn't have time to look for a vine. That hoopsnake was rolling along so close behind him now, the soles of his boots turned white with fright.

Andy dodged here, there, and yon, like a rabbit in a brush pile. The snake was slick and fat, and Andy figured it would have a hard time keeping up with a fellow as light of foot as he was.

But hoopsnakes, besides being mean, are nimble as weasels, and the snake didn't have any trouble zigzagging along behind Andy. It squeaked in and out among the trees right on Jackson's heels.

Once it nipped in close and struck with that black stinger oozing poison. Howsomever, it missed Andy and the stinger sank into a big tree. That tree just gave one quiver and fell over dead.

"Oh, oh," cried Andy to himself. "I must think of something to do quick, for my legs are young and inexperienced and they may get the habit of running so that they would never stop. And that would be bad for a lawyer who wants to do some fine great thing for people when he gets back to Nashville."

Now straight ahead of Andy rose a very steep hill, steep

as a hat on one side and even steeper on the other. And it came to him that the hill would be a help in getting rid of this snake.

He ran right at the hill and hit the slope, fairly churning up gravel, climbing for all he was worth. He drew a little ahead of the snake, for it was powerful fat and found rolling uphill troublesome.

When Andy got to the top, he left off running and turned around, dead still. And he didn't have long to wait, for here came the snake darting at Andy with its stinger ready.

Faster and faster rolled the snake, closer and closer with each whirling roll. It made Andy's heart quiver like a fledgling bird to stay there in the path of that varmint and not run. However, he stood his ground and never flinched, for he knew this was his only chance to best the hoopsnake.

And just as the snake was almost on him and its stinger was drawn back to strike, Andy jumped high in the air. The snake bowled underneath him, pretty as you please, just barely grazing the least little bottom piece of one of his boots.

And it rolled over the top and started down the other side of the hill. It went so fast, Andy couldn't even see it. He only knew it was traveling along because of the bushes flattened out behind it and the dead rabbits spewed out on all sides.

Quick as a wink it went whirling and bouncing and slamming down that hill and across the valley and up another hill on the other side.

The sight of it leaving him made Andy laugh. He whooped and hollered and slapped his leg and beat himself on the back to keep from choking. It was pleasant indeed to see that big varmint go whisking off, for there are few indeed who have ever outsmarted a hoopsnake.

Now the opposite hill was a very high one. The snake didn't quite roll all the way to the top of that one. It stopped a good thirty feet below the crest and rolled back the way it had come. Down the second hill it hurled, across the valley again, and back up the hillside straight at Andy Jackson.

When Andy saw it coming, he swallowed his laugh like it had been a mouthful of ice-cold briers. He gave a whoop loud enough to shake the hair off a 'possum's tail and jumped up to run.

But once again the snake stopped just before it reached the top of the hill and rolled back the way it had come, for you see it had long since lost the power to do anything for itself, but must just roll back and forth until it came to a stop.

Andy hollered at the Chief to come see, so the Indian climbed down and came running. He and Jackson watched the snake roll back and forth for quite a spell before they went on their way.

And later on, Andy heard from a man who lived nearby that the hoopsnake rolled for nearly a week. And at the end of that time when it stopped, it was worn down into a little tiny caterpillar and no more poisonous than a huckleberry.

But Andy and the Chief couldn't wait to see that. They had to hurry on. Andy started down the trail, but he noticed that something was the matter with one of his boots.

"Well, will you look at that?" he asked the Chief.

The boot that had grazed the hoopsnake was all black and shriveled. That's how poisonous hoopsnakes are.

The Chief told Andy to take off the boot quick before his toes caught the poison.

"This is the way Injuns take the poison out of a boot," he told the lawyer. And he washed it seven times in running creek water and made a cool poultice of sweet-gum balls and spotted cowbane to put on it.

Andy was mighty impatient to be gone, and he hated to wait long enough for the poultice to soak in good. "Ain't it been on there long enough?" he asked the Chief.

"Not near long enough," replied Chief Ticklepitcher.

"I believe he's just a-fooling me," thought Andy. "I don't reckon Injuns know such a heap much more about hoopsnakes than other folks. I believe that boot is ready to put on."

So he reached out to grab it, and there was so much poison left in that boot that it struck at Andy like a snake!

Andy was a little mite ashamed of himself, and he told the Chief so. "I won't never be hasty to doubt your word again," he promised. "For a fact, there is such a heap of things I don't know, it's hard for me sometimes to think what they are."

At last the Chief said the boot was safe, so Jackson eased his foot into it and it fitted pretty good. But the truth of the matter was, it never was much count after that. It was all drawn over on one side and discombobulated around the buckle.

Then off they hastened along the mountain trail, and the air grew sweeter and cooler, for East Tennessee is like that. And every kind of a September flower bloomed among the bushes—white snakeroot and blue monkshood and lavender bee balm and orange jewelweed. Oh, it was a mighty fine sight to behold, as bright as calico and as sweet smelling as a hay barn.

The trees were still as green as spring, and birds sang on every branch and water was everywhere, pouring down the rocky hillsides, spilling over falls, splashing into fern-lined pools.

Andy could hear the little springs grumbling to one another in the earth, "Lay over, lay over; oh, there ain't enough room down here."

The Chief got down off his horse and dug up one or two and wrapped them up in a snakeskin and stored them away in his saddlebag for use during another stretch of drought.

"I don't favor trying to take home springs," said Andy, shaking his head. "Springs are too little, and they're a terrible awkward shape to handle. Now it may be the easiest thing to do would be tie a rope around a river and drag it back home."

The Chief looked thoughtful-like. "I don't reckon you know these East Tennessee rivers like I do," he said. "They're a heap smaller than you think. And by the time you have shelled out the rocks, there wouldn't be so much left."

Andy nodded. "That's true, I can see," he agreed. "And we'd have to husk off the mud. Besides that, rivers and creeks are mighty wigglesome."

Chief Ticklepitcher figured a pond would be the easiest thing. They could find a big round one and roll it home.

"Now that's true as preaching," admitted Andy. "But folks around Nashville ain't much used to still water. As long as I've come all this way, I aim to do things right, so I'll fetch back a well."

"The very thing!" cried the Chief. "A well is easy to carry and seldom runs dry. Andy, you may not be an Injun, but you've got a powerful brain, all the same."

"Whip up your old horse then, and we'll ride fierce along this trail," said Andy, "for I aim to start back to Nashville this very day if things go right and we don't run into the Land Pirates or a plague of elks or something else bad."

And off he tore along the winding mountain path. The Chief followed along, and his blue blanket flapped out mightily behind him.

They asked at the very first cabin they reached, and the man told them a fellow named Blinky Bonesides had wells for sale, and he told them how to get there. Away they went again till they came to the top of a mountain and looked down. And there right below was a clearing with a cabin in it.

"That must be the place," Andy said.

They rode down and Andy knocked politely on the door. In a little spell a man came out of the cabin and said, "Howdy! I'm Blinky Bonesides, and howdy is what I say to strangers and friends alike. Howdy!" he roared again.

Then Andy explained who he was and how folks in Nashville were having such a monstrous bad drought and how he and the Chief had come there to buy a well from him.

The man slapped his leg. "You have most certainly come to the right place," he replied. "I got wells and wells. I got big ones and little ones, spickle, speckle, and spotted ones. And you shall have your pick, free of charge, for I hate to hear of folks in trouble, and I wouldn't take a cent for all the money in the world."

Andy thanked him mightily and shook his hand, and the Chief said even the Cherokees were not so generous and kind as Blinky Bonesides.

"Just let me get my hat and I'll show you the wells," Blinky told them. "They ain't but a whoop and a holler from here."

So he got his hat and led Andy and the Chief by the garden path and down a draw and through a cornfield and over a creek and up a crooked mountain to a big meadow.

And there they were, row on row of wells, every size and kind, all bright and sparkly.

"Now you can pick out any one you like excepting this one," Blinky told them, laying his hand on the well curb that stuck up above ground. "I wouldn't part with this one for a piggin of solid gold 'taters. Why, my young 'uns have had this one since they were tiny chaps, and they are plumb crazy about it. I guess it would just break their hearts to part with it."

"Oh, we wouldn't take that one for worlds," Andy cried. "How 'bout this one?"

"Oh, I'm sorry as I can be, but you can't have this well either," answered Blinky.

"What's wrong with this one?" asked Andy.

"Oh, there ain't nothing wrong with it," replied Blinky. "It's just that this is the onliest well the frogs will lay their eggs in."

"Frogs!" exclaimed Andy. "Whatever for do you need frogs, way back up here in the mountains, miles from anywhere?"

"Well, you see these here are kind of special frogs," Blinky explained. "They grow to right good size. And in the spring when I got a heap of little chickens and ducks, I put a few of these frogs around the place and they keep the hawks away from the biddies. When the frog sees a hawk come sailing overhead, he just jumps up in the air and swallows that hawk the way most frogs swallow flies. Now hawks is bad in these parts. And I wouldn't ever be able to raise any fowls without these frogs."

"Oh, well," said Andy, "we wouldn't want to work you any hardship. Though I tell you, folks around Nashville could sure use some of them frogs. Why, I've seen spring days over there when there were so many hawks in the sky, the sunlight couldn't get through to the ground. And it's a mighty lucky chicken that lives to be old enough to end up in the stewpot."

So Blinky promised to give Andy a few frogs to take home with him. And Andy and the Chief chose a well and pulled it up.

Then Andy and the Chief bade Blinky Bonesides farewell and picked up the well on their shoulders. Tying the horses behind, they hurried across the clearing and reached the trail. It was dim and lonesome there in the woods, but they set out toward Nashville with light steps.

Suddenly four men rose up out of the bushes and stood in the path. And the minute Andy saw them, he knew in reason they hadn't stopped him to ask how he was feeling.

And four less likely-looking men Andy had never clapped his two eyes on before. They were just exactly the kind of four men a body might expect to meet skinning a black cat in a graveyard at midnight, or at a very small hanging at a lonely crossroad. The sight of them made Andy's hair stand up as straight as the Carolina Militia.

Oh, he knew who they were! They were the famous Land Pirates, Mingo and Mango, and Big and Little Other-Brother. They were a horrid-looking bunch all right.

44

Mingo had two yellow fangs that came almost down to his Adam's apple, and one of his ears had been clipped off. Mango had one blue eye and one green, and the top of his head was gone where once a hungry horse had mistaken his hair for mouldy hay.

Big Other-Brother was little and bumpy like a cucumber, and Little Other-Brother was big and smooth like a catfish. And they had only one grin between them. When one started to grin, the other had to finish it, and so it was two times uglier and wickeder than any other grin in the world.

And all four of these Land Pirates carried knives and tomahawks and axes and pistols, clubs and swords and sawed-off fowling pieces and slingshots. You see they were the meanest kind of fellows, always ready to get into devilment and always well prepared for any sort of low-down wickedness.

"We'll take that well," said Mingo, who was the leader.

"I'd a heap rather take that red-headed feller and carve off his toes," said Mango.

"Well, we don't want you to. Do we, lambs?" Mingo asked the two Other-Brothers.

"Ask him," said Big Other-Brother, pointing at Little Other-Brother with a knife.

But Little Other-Brother didn't answer, for he hadn't been able to speak since he was born one cold December night.

"Tie a rope around it and we'll use their horses to drag

46

it off," ordered Mingo. "And be quick about it, my honeys."

The three Land Pirates had the well tied to the horses and ready to drag off before Andy and the Chief had time to say so much as one word, or move so much as one muscle, or eyelid, or kneecap.

Andy stepped forward.

"Now just a habeas corpus," he shouted, and that made the Land Pirates pause and look a little bit scared, for they didn't know what it meant at all. "There's no call for you to go taking my well. I need this well. There's a heap of water around and about here. If you want some water, you can go fetch it. Whatever would you want my well for?"

"You got it, ain't you?" snarled Mingo. "If you got it, we want to take it away from you."

And he whipped up the horses and away they dashed with the well. But Land Pirates aren't much good with wells and don't really know how to handle them. At the edge of the clearing the well struck a tree stump. One side was all smashed in.

Now a well has a heap of water in it, as any farmer's boy knows, and when it gets loose, there's liable to be trouble. A whole torrent of water came pouring out of the well, spreading out in every direction and carrying all things before it.

"Run for your life," shouted the Chief to Andy. "It's a flood!"

Four

The Chief ran like a canebrake afire. But Andy didn't run.

"For," he said to himself, "I can't run. I've done a heap of traveling today. I've run from hoopsnakes and I've got a bad boot. I've worked hard to get a water well for the folks at Nashville and it's all gone for naught. And now I'm a-getting mad. I can't run on account of I must stand here and keep a tight hold on my temper. And as soon as I get a good grip on my temper, then I'll be able to think of something helpful to do."

So Andy stood his ground while the water poured toward

49

him. He put his hands over his ears and squeezed hard to keep his temper from flying out that way. He squinched up his eyes and gritted his teeth and held in his temper the best way he knew how.

Now Andy glowed red hot from head to foot, just keeping his temper stoppered up inside him. Little heat waves went shooting out from him like sparks from an elm wood fire.

And all the while that wall of water came nearer and nearer, splashing and tumbling and booming among the rocks and thickets. It swirled up pig pens and skillets, feather beds and stone chimneys and just a heap of big old water-logged mosquitoes.

And then the flood came sweeping up to Andy, but it never got close. While it was still three feet away, that water turned to steam from the terrible heat generated by Andy's bottled-up temper.

There was a hissing and sizzling like snakes going to church. Steam went up in puffs and streams and clouds, and soon the whole Cumberland Mountains were covered with mist and all the coves and valleys and hollows were filled with fog.

Howsomever, the water cooled down Andy's temper considerably, though it happened so quickly the shock was almost more than a decent feller like him could bear. And he just stood there for a while a-shivering and a-shaking like he had the ague.

Now Chief Ticklepitcher, being an Injun, could see in a fog most nigh as well as he could in the dark, so he made haste to fetch the horses from where they were still tied to the empty shell of the old well. The critters were skittish as gadflies, for they could smell the Land Pirates bumbling about in the mist.

"What on earth will we do now?" asked the Chief when he had come up to Andy and the lawyer had felt him all over to make sure it really was the Chief and not a tree that had started walking around.

Andy gave one last shiver and began to think.

"We'll just have to go get us another well," he answered. "But I'm much afeared that first we'll have to do something about this fog, for it is so thick that creatures like tadpoles and hellgrammites that ain't got much sense will not know where the creek stops and the fog starts. And first thing we know the air will be full of all manner of varmints that ought to be in creeks and ponds, and they will be a terrible nuisance."

The Chief nodded, for he had already spied a big old snapping turtle sitting on a limb of a chestnut tree.

"We'll go back to Blinky Bonesides', for it may be he knows a good remedy for too much fog," Andy went on. "Though I declare if the stuff wasn't so wet, it would make the best kind of stuffing for beds and pillows and a fellow could grow rich selling it to folks."

The Chief looked all around for the Land Pirates, but he couldn't spy them anywhere. "I reckon they're hid out some-

51

where," said Andy. "Maybe they won't bother us no more, for I don't think they aimed for that well-stealing to turn out the way it did."

Chief Ticklepitcher found the trail, and they made their way back to Blinky's. Andy was thankful to find that the well-owner and his family were all safe as daisies because the flood had missed their farm entirely.

"I clean forgot to warn you about Mingo and his gang being close around here," Blinky told Andy. "They are the meanest varmints in all creation, I do believe. They ain't even fit to be cut up for catfish bait."

"Well, there's no use crying over burnt ashcake," said Andy. "Right now we got to figure out something to do about this here fog. And I kind of had the notion we could stuff most of it in that hole we left when we pulled up the well."

Blinky slapped his leg. "That's the very thing!" he cried.

"You could put a good stout cover over the hole," went on Andy. "And next summer when you and your boys are hoeing corn and the sun gets powerful strong and hot, you can fetch up a heap of the fog and spread it around over the fields to make shade."

Now Blinky was plumb delighted to hear this, you may be sure, for his cornfields were often so sunny and hot, hoe blades just melted and sank into the ground.

And Andy was glad to be a help to him. He and the Chief and Blinky and Blinky's two oldest boys went out to the spot where the well had been pulled up, and it wasn't long till they had that hole filled up to the brim with thick fog.

Then Blinky's boys jumped into the hole and trampled the fog down good till there was a heap more room. And the others pulled and poked more fog in and Blinky's boys stomped that down good, and pretty soon almost every bit of the fog was packed tight in that wellhole. And the day was sunny and bright again.

While Blinky was making a big wooden cover for the hole, Andy fretted because he was anxious to get a second well and get started back to Nashville.

"For you see," he told the Chief in a low voice, "while I'm gone some other body might come along and think up some powerful good thing to do for the folks there. Why, right this minute he may be writing out statutes and passing ordinances. Now I have counted a heap on being the one to do some real fine thing for those folks, and if I don't get to do it, it will be a terrible disappointment."

The Chief said he could see how that was. Just about that

time Blinky hollered for them to come ahead and pick out another well.

So Andy jumped up and trotted up and down the rows of wells, hoping he could find another as good as the first he had picked. He felt of them and plunked them with his fingers.

"How about this one at the very bottom here?" he asked.

Blinky clapped Andy on the shoulder. "The very one!" he exclaimed. "Not too big and not too little. And the water's clear and sweet and cool. You've picked a fine one, lawyer."

So Andy bunged up the top of the well, and the Chief got some big grapple hooks and they put the hooks into the well curb. Then very slowly they began to pull the well up out of the ground using the horses to help. Blinky went and got a couple of mules, but even so, it was hard work this time.

It took just a heap of pulling and shouting and tugging and sweating to get that well up out of the ground. Once they had it about halfway out and it slipped off the hooks and fell back in place in the hole.

Andy had a terrible struggle to hold his temper then. He worked at it so hard he had to be blanketed and rubbed down like a horse.

But at last the task was done and they eased the well down on the ground, working slow and careful, for wells are sometimes brittle as new-blown glass flasks.

The well wasn't chipped or cracked or anything. Andy was mighty proud to see it lying there on the ground, full to bursting with tasty water.

"That's a fine well and we're mighty grateful to you," he told Blinky.

"Why, it ain't nothing a-tall," Blinky replied. "I'm proud to help out the folks over yonder at Nashville. And I owe you a heap of thanks for getting that fog stored away in that hole. I aim to use that fog for many a long year to come."

So Blinky and Andy shook hands, and Andy and the Chief heaved the well to their shoulders and started off with the horses following. They looked everywhere for the Land Pirates, but there wasn't a sign of them.

Andy had made up his mind the Pirates shouldn't steal this well, so he looked mighty keen at every tree and bush they came to, for he didn't want to be surprised again.

After a while Andy stopped and said, "This here well must be a fine one. I declare it's even heavier than the first one. Let's shift to the other shoulder awhile."

So they changed shoulders and went off again. Andy reckoned he'd never in his life felt such a weight as now bore down on him. It pushed down on him so much that soon he sank into the ground up to his knees with every step he took. Every time he stepped on a pebble he mashed it till the juices squirted out.

"This will never do," he told the Chief, for he'd begun to be a mite suspicious. "Let's put this well down and have a look at it, for I believe to my soul there's some rabbits roosting on top."

So Jackson and Chief Ticklepitcher began to lower the

well to the ground slowly, for it was slippery and smooth and right hard to hold.

"Why, I believe I do see something on top of it, sure enough," said Andy, twisting his neck to see up on top of the well.

"Likely it's an owl with its feathers all washed away," commented the Chief. "Fogs is mortal hard on owls."

They lowered the well a little bit more. "Whatever there is, there's four of it," exclaimed Andy.

"Maybe it's the measles trying to get to Nashville this here way," suggested the Chief. "Measles has to travel some way, you know."

Then the well rested on the ground and Andy straightened up. And four men stepped off the well and stood there before Andy right on the path.

"Why, it's the Land Pirates," moaned Andy. "They been riding on top and we never saw so much as a toe of them."

"We'll take that well and you two beauties to boot," snarled Mingo.

And he laughed a laugh that sent shivers racing around Andy's ribs.

Five

"Now hold on a minute here," cried Andy. "This is my well,
all legal and lawful. And I say you can't have it."

Mango gave a happy snarl. "Oh, I've got a big old knife
says we can have it. And I got a little knife says we got to
have it. And I got a middle-sized knife says we *will* have it."

And he jerked all three of them out of his belt and juggled
them up in the air, never so much as taking his eyes off Andy
once.

Chief Ticklepitcher began to undo the knot in his long
hair. A screech owl and two turkeys flew out with a terrible
commotion.

"Put them knives up, Mango," ordered Mingo. "You might cut somebody accidental-like. Mightn't he, my loveys?" he asked the Other-Brothers.

But they didn't say anything, just stood there sulking all the while.

Chief Ticklepitcher undid some more of his hair, and a three-legged skillet and just a whole heap of dry leaves fell out.

"And I wouldn't want anybody to get hurt, would I, honeys?" Mingo asked.

He pointed at Andy. "I do dearly love to hear a red-headed lawyer talk better'n anybody in the world," he said. "We got a couple of hours to spare before we take this well away from you, and I would like to hear you say something else, for your voice is as soothing as the sound of a catamount sharpening its claws on a limestone cliff."

And he grinned a wide grin, showing a heap more jagged yellow fangs than Andy cared about inspecting.

Just about that time the Chief undid the last bit of his big old knot of hair. Two horn spoons and some spiders and his bow and arrow tumbled down.

Quick as midday light the Chief snatched up the arrow and fitted it to his bow. Now he had counted a heap on sending that arrow flying right through all four of the Land Pirates. But the dampness had bent the arrow out of shape, and the Chief knew it would never in this world hit what he aimed at, all curved in the middle that way.

Howsomever, Andy knew a good thing when he saw it and he was mighty quick to figure out a way to use that arrow. He grabbed up a good stout rope he had and tied it to the feather end of the arrow.

"Quick, Chief, shoot!" he cried.

Chief Ticklepitcher drew back the bowstring and fired it off. Of course, being bent just that way, the arrow didn't take a straight course. It curved. And the Chief, being an Injun, knew how to make it curve just exactly right.

Round and round it went with that rope trailing along behind it. And before you could say "Land Grant" or "Tombigbee Territory," that arrow had caught those Land Pirates up in a bunch and tied them up rope-tight.

"Chief Ticklepitcher, you shot just exactly right," Andy told him. And he ran to catch up the ends of the rope and make an even tighter knot in it.

Now the rope had caught Mingo and Mango around the waist, and Little Other-Brother around the knees, for he was so big. But Big Other-Brother was so small the rope had only gone around the last bump on top of his head. He gave a wiggle and a shake and slipped out of the rope.

And he didn't stay to shake hands all around—he just up and ran off down the trail like a rabbit who doesn't care a whang about being a wildcat's dinner.

"I'll get him," shouted Andy, and he took off lickety-cut after Big Other-Brother.

Big Other-Brother couldn't run too good, for he had grass-

hopper-high knees and a mighty low chin and he kept knocking himself down on a fast straight stretch. When he saw that Andy was catching up with him, he ran off the path and crawled in among the bushes where some monstrous big toadstools were growing.

He crouched down among them, and the fact was he looked mighty like one of them. But Andy's eyes were as sharp as his nose, and he very soon spied the Land Pirate by the red bandana tied around his neck.

"Oh, ho, I've got you," yelled Andy as he threw himself forward.

But Big Other-Brother scuttled away among the trees till he came to a great wide ravine with a whole heap of sharp jagged rocks at the bottom. With Andy Jackson flying through the woods behind him, Big Other-Brother yearned greatly to see the sights upon the far side. Without so much as a pause, he gathered himself up and sailed out into space.

Andy had never been a powerful jumper, for a fact. "But if a Land Pirate can jump that far, a lawyer can do it," he thought, and he wound himself up tight and let loose.

Howsomever, he was not much more than halfway across when he saw he couldn't make it. "I'll have to go back and let Big Other-Brother get away," he told himself.

So Andy turned in a gentle curve, as graceful as a swallow on a summer's evening, and he headed back over the ravine the way he had come.

He looked back at Big Other-Brother and he saw plain

that the Land Pirate wasn't going to make it across either. But Big Other-Brother didn't have sense enough to figure out how to turn back in mid-air that way. He whipped around, quick as scat, sharp as a needle, and broke his left leg at the ankle. Andy could hear it snap in two.

Then of course, with one leg broken and useless, Big Other-Brother couldn't go a step further. He just sort of hung in the air for a minute and then went tumbling down in among the rocks, yelling and screeching, and nobody ever saw him again.

But Andy landed safely on the spot he had jumped from. And he made haste back to help the Chief tie up the rest of the Land Pirates.

And oh, what a terrible sight to see! What an awful frightening thing had happened! The Land Pirates had escaped from the rope and were playing a most terrible game with Chief Ticklepitcher.

They had tied the Chief to a tree with his very own rope. And they were slashing at his legs something awful with knives and swords and axes and every kind of sharp-cutting thing. Mingo was even biting at him with his big old yellow fangs.

Chief Ticklepitcher had to jump and skip and hop and wiggle like a cricket at a house-raising to keep from having his toes lopped clear off.

"Ho, ho," sang Mango. "I aim to carve up this here Injun, just a little bit every day and a good-sized piece put by for tomorrow. Oh, ain't I the cruelest in the world?"

Now that made Andy riled, you may be sure. And he began to roll up his sleeves. "Chief Ticklepitcher is my friend and I don't aim to lose him," he said to himself.

"Hee, hee," whooped Mingo. "You ain't as mean as me. As soon as you finish off that Injun, I aim to take this well to Nashville. And when I get in sight of the town, I'll let the water flow out into the dust and not give the folks one drop of it. Ain't that mean, mean, mean?"

And he gnashed his fangs at the Chief once again as he danced by.

Andy's hackles were a-rising fast, for a fact.

Little Other-Brother said nothing, for he couldn't. But he had a knife that could talk mighty sharp, and he flung it straight at the Chief's head and cut off three or four of his eyelashes and a handful of his war paint.

Now Andy had stood just about as much as a body can stand.

"This takes the rag off the bush," bawled Andy. "And I ain't holding back no more. Right this minute my temper is swelling up inside me like hot cider in a tight barrel and the staves are about to bust loose. I aim to get mad, and those that ain't got a good stout roof over their heads had better seek shelter quick."

And then Andy got mad sure enough, for he knew the right time had come.

Six

Now Andy had held his temper so long, it was most nigh muscle-bound. It took a minute or two to really-let loose. And for a tiny little spell he hummed and bumbled like a bee under a dinner bell.

Then he wound up like a clock and whirled in one spot till the dust flew. There was a sudden shooosh, and Andy's temper was loose and running wild all over the Cumberland Mountains.

He roared and whooped and stomped and stormed. Hollow trees were flattened into boards, saplings were chewed into splinters, and sawdust was flung all over creation. And when that was done, Andy went to bawling and bellowing and bang-

ing and whanging. Rocks were caved in with one blow and mole tunnels were turned inside out.

Trees were blown down every which a way, creeks stopped running, and roads turned around and went the other way. But he kept right on. He twirled and kicked; he swooped and sashayed around, and his arms spun about as fast as a spider in a thunderstorm.

A big flock of passenger pigeons was so frightened, they lost the power of flight and had to walk from Tennessee to south-central Alabama. Foxes turned white in their dens, and it was ten years before any more mushrooms grew in that section of the country.

Chief Ticklepitcher had to admire Andy. He'd seen the lawyer lose his temper before, but never anywhere near so far as this. He laughed as hard as anybody can with their eyelashes all gone, for Andy had sense enough to miss him and the horses and the well.

There were gusts of wind, and squirrels came flying out of their holes. Black clouds gathered in the sky, and the ground stretched like hot taffy.

Now the Land Pirates didn't know about Jackson's temper. They saw all those trees coming down and the dust rising, heard all that roaring and ranting, and it was too much for them.

"Lambs!" screamed Mingo. "It's the world's worst hurricane, along with two-three earthquakes and a blizzard. Run for your lives!"

So they all took to their heels. But Andy ripped into them with such a blast, he blew the whole lot into a six-gallon jug. And when he had calmed down, he put a stopper in the jug and sent it rolling off to the High Sheriff.

You can bet Andy was cut up some from all that commotion and pretty worn out too. The Chief made a poultice of cobwebs and charcoal and the least last leaves of rattlesnake fern. He smeared this over the gashes and used Andy's shirttail to bind them up with.

"I knowed a medicine doctor bound up a cut on a man's nose with dog hair once," said the Chief, "and ever afterwards that man ran after rabbits just like a hound."

Andy didn't worry much over that, for he was a lawyer and

had little time to chase rabbits, though it did seem like a mighty pleasant way to spend your free time.

Jackson might have rested there all that day and that night, for he was mighty weak. All his strength had got down in the bottom of his stockings, and it was a good thing they didn't have any holes in them, for otherwise his strength might have spilled out and been lost forever.

But while he was lying on the ground, resting and gathering himself together around the edges, he saw a very curious thing—one man riding on another man's shoulders.

"Howdy!" cried Andy Jackson to the man underneath. "Is your friend hurt bad?"

"Nope," answered the man underneath, "he ain't hurt at all."

"Is he sick?" asked Andy.

"Nope," said the man underneath. "He's fine as kine."

"Well, then, why in the nation are you toting him on your shoulders?" yelled Andy.

"I'll tell you why, stranger," replied the man riding on the other man's shoulders. "You see this feller here has the rheumatism mighty bad. He's a big man as you can see, and it got so bad his legs wouldn't hold him up. 'My legs is no use to me,' says he, and I says, 'I'm a little lightweight feller, and I reckon I could use your legs nicely.' And he says, 'How much?' and I says, 'Six bits.' So when I take a journey or go anywheres that's some distance off, I use his legs and save my own."

"Oh," said Andy. "And where are you journeying to now?"

"Anywhere!" cried the man on top. "Anywhere to get away from Nashville and that dry weather. I can't stand it no more."

"Folks ain't leaving Nashville, are they?" exclaimed Andy. "Why, I'm fetching water to them this very minute."

"Well," said the man, "I don't know about other folks, but I'm leaving. Giddup there, John's legs."

And away they went, the little man using big John's legs.

Now Andy, all tizzified as he was, got to his feet. "Them pore folks have got to have help," he said. "It don't matter how I feel, we have got to get on with this water well."

Andy looked the well over carefully to make sure he hadn't hurt it any with his temper. But it was in fine shape.

"Quick, now, Chief, let's heave it up and be gone," Andy said, taking hold of one end.

But of course he couldn't carry it a step. He was still too weak to tote a load, so they had to let Andy's old black horse carry the back end. It was mighty cumbersome for him walking on his hind legs, but he managed it for Andy's sake.

And away they went. Andy rode on the Chief's horse, and as he rode, he chewed sourwood leaves and sassafras roots and slippery elm bark and black gum twigs, so his strength came oozing slowly back into him.

Along the winding trail they went and down the mountainside to the valley. Andy rode ahead and called out where there were roots and stones that might trip the well-toters. By and by he came to a big old creek.

It was just the kind of creek Andy liked best, full of minnows and rocks and crawdads and baby catfish and water cress, with a little waterfall all the way across. But where the trail crossed the creek, there was a long quiet pool.

Andy was a mite worried, for this is just the kind of creek that snapping turtles are apt to like best too. And as he studied the water, he saw a heap of bubbles come rising up from the creek's bottom. He had a notion that right in that very spot there might be some of the snappingest sort of turtles.

He told the Chief what he suspicioned, and the Chief agreed.

"We'll hold the well way up where they can't get hold of it," Chief Ticklepitcher said. "And I misdoubt any old snapper'll try to grab me or the horses, for I'll rub us all over with a mite of goose grease, and if there's anything a turtle can't abide, it's cold goose grease."

Andy figured it might be a good idea to rub the grease on the well's sides too. But the Chief only had a little gourdful, and when he'd rubbed it on him and the horses, there wasn't any left for the well.

"We'll hold it up high," he promised Andy. "Don't you worry none. We'll get over all right."

So Chief Ticklepitcher waded out into the stream and Andy's old black horse followed, and they toted the well between them. Everything went fine and dandy and they were almost across when the old black horse slipped and fell. The bottom was mighty slick, and he just wasn't used to walking on his hind legs that way.

Down he came with a crash and a smash, and the well rolled into the water as neat as a pin. The Chief made haste to drag it out and Andy rushed to help, but it was too late.

"Oh, I'm afeared one's got it, Andy!" the Chief cried.

And sure enough there was a big old snapping turtle holding onto the well on one side and an even bigger one holding to the other side. They rolled their sharp eyes at Andy and gritted their jaws tight.

"Oh, forevermore!" exclaimed Andy. "Now these here fool varmints won't let go till it thunders, and that's liable to be next June. We must just take them on to Nashville with us."

The Chief hitched both horses to the well, and he and the beasts heaved and pulled, while Andy pushed at the rear. Howsomever, they couldn't budge those turtles a 'coon's hair. The critters just dug their toes way down in the roots of the mud and hung on.

"We'll just have to think of something else," said Andy, and he pondered fiercely. "If I wasn't so all-fired weak, I could make a little thunder myself," he added.

He thought a bit more and then he said, "I'll tell you what I'll do. I'll tell a funny tale, and when the turtles open their jaws to laugh, you and the horses pull for all you're worth and get the well out of the creek before they know what's going on."

So the Chief got all set and Andy harrumphed a time or two and then he began. "I had a bald-headed friend once who was very easy to see through, for he had a big old pain in his stomach."

The Chief chuckled and the horses nodded their heads, but the turtles never even smiled.

Andy waited a minute and then he tried again. "I knowed two brothers once and they looked just alike, but one of them was uglier than the other, for he had only one eye so he could only look half as good."

Chief Ticklepitcher busted out laughing and the horses neighed, but the turtles clamped down on the well all the

75

harder.

Andy was desperate and he thought terribly hard. Then he yelled out, "I knowed a big old hairy man once who bought a hat, and he said it must be a straw hat, for it couldn't be felt!"

Still the turtles didn't laugh.

But the Chief laughed so much he fell in the creek and got water up his nose and had to be hauled out and squeezed dry and pounded hard on the back.

"I reckon that won't work," said Andy sadly. But he didn't give up, for he'd learned on this journey to keep trying, though in truth he hardly knew what to do next.

But all of a sudden he recollected something, and a big grin spread over his face. He whispered to Chief Tickle-pitcher. The Chief nodded and grinned too, for he was certain-sure this time they'd get away from those turtles.

Now Andy sat astraddle the well with feet dangling down, one right over each turtle. He had something clenched tight in each fist, and when he saw the Chief and the horses were ready to pull, he leaned down and opened his fists right over each turtle's nose, and something sprinkled down.

It was the pepper he'd ground up in his pepper mill just before he left Nashville!

Well, those turtles squirmed and twitched and sneered, trying every which way not to sneeze. But it wasn't any use. That pepper was fresh and as strong as a buckeyed calf, and in just a minute or two the turtles' jaws flew open.

"Pull!" screamed Andy. "Pull hard!"

And the Chief pulled, along with the horses. And in no time the well was free and lying out on the bank, while the turtles were churning up the water, sneezing and snuffling and snorting like all git-out.

Andy looked back once as they set off, and he saw the turtles were mad but not too bad off, and that was good, for he never went to hurt them. It's just a snapping turtle's way to snap and he doesn't mean any harm by it.

The travelers went along slowly on account of Andy still wasn't too pert and could only relieve them for a short spell at a time. And it took a night and part of another day to get back to Nashville. But nobody or nothing bothered them, and they had water aplenty to drink and keep cool with.

Along about the middle of the day, they rode into Nashville. Folks had heard they were coming, and everybody was gathered in the square with piggins and kettles and noggins and open mouths and sop rags.

And oh, how they took on when they saw Andy and the water well! They shouted and sang and hurrahed like it was Christmas and Fourth of July on the same day.

Andy divided out the water, and there was a gracious plenty of it. Every man jack of them, and every woman and young 'un too, had water to drink and to cook with, water to go on the gardens and fields, water to prime springs and creeks to get them to running again, and still there was water to spare.

One or two even washed with some of the water.

When at last the water was gone, Andy cut up the well to make bee gums, and they made the finest hives and the best honey ever seen.

Andy made a short speech about how glad he was to be able to bring the water to them, how generous Blinky Bonesides had been, what a great help Chief Eight Shillings Six Pence Ticklepitcher had been, and he told how he planned to get rid of the rest of the dry weather.

And then the folks picked Andy Jackson up on their shoulders and paraded around the square and hollered some more.

"Now, here," exclaimed Andy. "There ain't no call to take on so. Put me down, for I'm anxious to get back to my law books and find some fine great thing to do for you good folks."

"Why, Andy," cried a man, "you've done the finest, greatest thing a body could do for us."

"Me?" asked Andy in surprise. "I just fetched back the water like you asked me too."

"Oh, Andy," answered the man. "That was the finest, greatest thing you could ever have done for us right now. It was a hard thing to do and a brave thing, and you did it for us just when we needed to have you do it."

Then Andy saw. He saw that to help folks out, you must do what needs to be done the worst way. When people need a specially good spondulacious law written—why, that is the thing to do right then and there. But when they need water —why, the finest, grandest thing to do is to fetch them some water.

"Well, forevermore," said Andy, for there had been such a power of things he didn't know, and now he'd learned such a lot.

And when all the cheering and celebrating was done, Andy went back to his cabin and his law books. And Chief Ticklepitcher went back to his dusting and polishing, toting and fetching. And all the folks of Nashville went back to farming and hunting and fishing and living.

And they do say that Andy Jackson helped out the folks every way he knew how after that. They say he even got to be President of the United States, but I don't know. It may be just a tall tale.